Advance Praise for

AN ALMOST PURE EMPTY WALKING

"Tryfon Tolides has followed the territory set out in his native Greece by C. P. Cavafy and later followed (in geography and sensibility) by Jack Gilbert. But Tolides trades the darkness of those poets for a more illuminated grandeur. Tolides is the shaman of epiphany. He makes for his reader keen and particular moments of revelation seized from his fierce and fleshly occupancy on the planet. In the wide-eyed consolation these poems offer up, the starlight they emit, he conjures Tomas Transtromer and other poets of profound spiritual power. At a time when the planet is in flames, he gives being human a good name." —MARY KARR

"How he surprises us—this young Greek poet—again and again in these brilliant, Chaplinesque, Zen-soaked, Vermeer-like cameos, craftily echoing Cavafy and William Carlos Williams and Gilbert and others. In the things of this world, which we so often fail to notice, Tolides finds worlds within words, pulling them out of his gypsy bag and holding them up to the light like the tiny diamonds they are, one after the other: the door, the dogs, the barbed wire fence, the dying mother, the holy air. This is his first book and already he has managed to stake out himself—and for us— a brand new, ancient, brave new world." —PAUL MARIANI

"It takes a skillful musician, or a poet, to play quietly. Tryfon Tolides's poems have the authority of a pitchless whisper, which lets his readers hear the sounds that are intimate, tender, wounded. His poetic undertaking takes places against two axes: the horizontal journey of civilizations from Greece to the U.S. and the vertical axis, which reaches from underground to the mysteries of the air." —BRUCE SMITH

"Because he sees with the humility of a searching heart, on the path to the spring in the village where he was born, on his pizza delivery route in small-town USA, Tryfon Tolides sees us as we are, as souls on pilgrimage in the world. The depth of this attention makes his poems not just consummations of the skill of his extraordinary mind, but revelations of the consequence of being." —BROOKS HAXTON

"Lost between his old life in a Greek village and his new life in America, Tryfon Tolides describes the mysteries of the new place and the increasing strangeness of the world he has left behind. Imagistic, interrogative, and often moving, these are the poems in which he finds himself, bringing a fresh and compelling voice to our poetry." —WESLEY MCNAIR

"Tryfon Tolides has written a wonderful book. The poems in *An Almost Pure Empty Walking* consolidate a quiet in me. There is a disarming range of tone and character, and characters, among the poems. Imaginative, political, provocative. But quiet." —MICHAEL BURKARD

PENGUIN BOOKS

AN ALMOST PURE EMPTY WALKING

TRYFON TOLIDES was born in Korifi Voiou, Greece. He lives and writes in Farmington, Connecticut. He has completed a BFA in Creative Writing at the University of Maine, and a MFA at Syracuse University. He had received a Reynolds Scholarship and the 2004 Foley Poetry Prize.

THE NATIONAL POETRY SERIES

The National Poetry Series was established in 1978 to ensure the publication of five poetry books annually through participating publishers. Publication is funded by the Lannan Foundation; the late James A. Michener and Edward J. Piszek through the Copernicus Society of America; Stephen Graham; International Institute of Modern Letters; Joyce & Seward Johnson Foundation; Juliet Lea Hillman Simonds Foundation; Tiny Tiger Foundation; and, Charles B. Wright III. This project also is supported in part by an award from the National Endowment for the Arts, which believes that a great nation deserves great art.

2005 COMPETITION WINNERS

Steve Gehrke of Columbia, Missouri, *Michelangelo's Seizure*
Chosen by T. R. Hummer, to be published by University of Illinois Press

Nadine Meyer of Columbia, Missouri, *The Anatomy Theater*
Chosen by John Koethe, to be published by HarperCollins Publishers

Patricia Smith of Tarrytown, New York, *Teahouse of the Almighty*
Chosen by Edward Sanders, to be published by Coffee House Press

S. A. Stepanek of West Chicago, Illinois, *Three, Breathing*
Chosen by Mary Ruefle, to be published by Verse Press/Wave Books

Tryfon Tolides of Farmington, Connecticut, *An Almost Pure Empty Walking*
Chosen by Mary Karr, to be published by Penguin Books

AN ALMOST PURE
EMPTY WALKING

TRYFON TOLIDES

PENGUIN BOOKS

PENGUIN BOOKS

Published by the Penguin Group
Penguin Group (USA) Inc., 375 Hudson Street,
New York, New York 10014, U.S.A.
Penguin Group (Canada), 90 Eglinton Avenue East, Suite 700,
Toronto, Ontario, Canada M4P 2Y3 (a division of Pearson Penguin Canada Inc.)
Penguin Books Ltd, 80 Strand, London WC2R 0RL, England
Penguin Ireland, 25 St Stephen's Green, Dublin 2,
Ireland (a division of Penguin Books Ltd)
Penguin Group (Australia), 250 Camberwell Road,
Camberwell, Victoria 3124, Australia (a division of Pearson Australia Group Pty Ltd)
Penguin Books India Pvt Ltd, 11 Community Centre,
Panchsheel Park, New Delhi - 110 017, India
Penguin Group (NZ), cnr Airborne and Rosedale Roads, Albany,
Auckland 1310, New Zealand (a division of Pearson New Zealand Ltd)
Penguin Books (South Africa) (Pty) Ltd, 24 Sturdee Avenue,
Rosebank, Johannesburg 2196, South Africa

Penguin Books Ltd, Registered Offices:
80 Strand, London WC2R 0RL, England

First published in Penguin Books 2006

1 3 5 7 9 10 8 6 4 2

LIBRARY OF CONGRESS CATALOGING IN PUBLICATION DATA
Tolides, Tryfon.
An almost pure empty walking / Tryfon Tolides.
p. cm.—(National poetry series)
ISBN 0 14 30.3709 9
I. Title. II. Series.
PS3620.O328A79 2006
811'.6—dc22   2005058617

Printed in the United States of America
Set in Goudy   •   Designed by Sabrina Bowers

For the memory of my parents:
PANAGIOTI AND ZOI

And for my brother:
DEMETRI

ACKNOWLEDGMENTS

America: "The Mouse and the Human"

Atlanta Review: "Circus," "From Mount Athos"

Creative Juices: "Early April Evening"

Kaleidoscope: "A Perfect Day" "Watering"

Limestone: "The Third One"

Long Island Quarterly: "Delivery"

Mondo Greco: "Agora"

Nota Bene: "By the Pier"

Sierra Nevada College Review: "A Doctor's Analogy," "Bone Marrow Biopsy"

Worcester Review: "Siesta"

Thanks to my teachers: Edward Ifkovic, Steve Straight, Elizabeth Cooke, Alice Bloom, Wes McNair, Dan Gunn, Pat O'Donnel, Brooks Haxton, Bruce Smith, Michael Burkard, Bob Gates, and Mary Karr. *Thanks* also to the National Poetry Series, and to Paul Slovak and Penguin Books.

CONTENTS

A little farther
we will see the almond trees blossoming
the marble gleaming in the sun
the sea breaking into waves

a little farther,
let us rise a little higher

—George Seferis, from *Mythistorema*
(translated by Edmund Keeley
and Philip Sherrard)

They were those from the wilderness of stars . . .

—Wallace Stevens

AN ALMOST PURE
EMPTY WALKING

IMMIGRANT

My mother called this morning, kept trailing away,
or off, with complaints about her failure
to make it, alone in the house, the night being
long, no one to talk to, blaming, in part, America,
hating the mess we've found, or made this year.
"What is America?" she said. "A hole in the water.
What have we gained but poison and illness?"
Her whole message, a cry, though still she asked
what I would eat for lunch. Back in bed,
I listened awhile to the furnace. Then, dressed,
passed the same books and papers spread on the floor,
and out, to the snow, the crows in the park.

ALMOND TREE

I miss smashing the green-covered shells,
peeling the bitter skin, putting the slippery seed
on my tongue.

I miss the outhouse. I miss the wind blowing
through the hole in the floor.

I miss the small door to the fallen balcony
and the swallows' nests and their tunnels
stuck to the stone.

I miss the smell of fried eggs, potatoes, and cheese.

I miss the wood-paneled radio with the voices
from Tirane and Skopje.

I miss the dogs at midnight and the church gates
and the steep forest behind the cemetery.

I miss the bundles of tree limbs, the crackling fires,
the crazy bright fields of tan and clover.

I miss going down hills on wood sleds
made from old chairs, greased with pig lard.

I miss the barbed wire fence around the orchard
and climbing the cherry trees and watching ants
on the bark and flicking them off my fingers.

I miss the spring water. I miss the plug to the tap
to the spring water, the cloth and wood.

I miss the walk to the spring. I miss the black sky.
I miss the ghosts in the holy air.

CIRCUS

Once, when I was little,
some gypsies came to the village.

It was a hot Aegean rock-burning sun,
a hot dry fields-on-fire day.

The road was dust at midnoon—
while iron bars latched shutters, and people slept
and bees and flies patrolled the flowers
and lizards spat underneath slate
and winds stirred waves of weeds
across the cemetery.

The gypsies would pass through like comets,
restrapping old chairs, selling embroidered
tablecloths, fine rugs, fresh fruit.
The tented pickup made its way
through neighborhood narrows and hands and offers,
and village women in pocketed aprons would emerge
from their houses, as if for the first time,
curious and shy, suspicious, welcoming.

Our mothers sometimes threatened
to give us to the gypsies,
who would bundle us away in their silk bolts
to the distant bazaars,
to sell us in streets, under canopies.

The heat grew like vines that day,
and in a short grass field, bangles of gypsy women
in veils with gold-toothed smiles,
and kicks that spun the earth on its side.
Clarinets and big skin drums played,

3

and sweat was the shine on faces,
and cats made for the shadow of the quince tree
when suddenly, the circles collapsed into a crowd,
and cheer evaporated,
and voices silenced above a fainted gypsy man.

Someone disappeared toward the well,
and God returned him quickly,
with a pail of water.
Then the gypsy's eyes splashed open,
and cracks of laughter resprung along the hillsides,
and the bare feet of gypsy children resumed their dance,
the air filled with the deep boom of drums.

THE FIRST THING: *OUSIA*

At first, it is one thing. Insignificant and supreme. The first thing.
You develop ways around it. Never solve it. It becomes part of you.
Years pass. Another thing comes. You think: if only I can solve
this new thing, if it will only go away, because the first has become
livable somewhat, with held breaths, and luck (though, truly, you don't
want to have the first thing, because it remains dangerous).
But by the time you think it through, the new thing becomes part
of your nerves. Then, more things pile up. And so, more held breaths,
more luck hoped for. You try to find value in it. In my village,
they say certain pears are best eaten after they've fallen to the ground
and been there a few days, their bruises grown. The fruit attains its fullest
flavor then, just as with certain soups, you have to suck the bones
of their marrow to get the *ousia*, the essence, the best part.

ETYMOLOGICAL

The word *cancer* was like a candy wrapper
from a country I'd almost heard of.
Karkinos in Greek. Close to *kokkinos*,
red. The k makes the crust and scab of the word.
The r the rich tube-like liquid,
possibly to ooze or stain or bulge. In the clinic

above the busy intersection in Thessaloniki.
My Uncle Apostolos' bed
was white. What I remember of the word *cancer*
when the dark of it first dissolved into being:
the metal bed frame was painted white
and round above his head. The sheets had some red
toward his feet, near his stomach. I looked at his face
to see how he was carrying the heavy word,
to see what such a word on a face looked like.
The nurses' shoes made cold urgent clock sounds.

When I walked onto the balcony to lean
my hands on the rail and over, I heard cars below
in the streets, horns and brakes, the mixing voices
of people. A waiter could be carrying
espresso and water on a brass tray to a small round blue
table with a man and a woman waiting.

ALL SUMMER

I go to a spring in my village,
carrying two white plastic jugs
along the steep path
to the base of the mountain,
by the sparrowed wild fruit tree.
Cold water rushes into my hand,
where my face dips, and I fill
my belly like a horse's belly,
then the jugs with their sound
of empty space escaping,
and I bring them past graves
around the church, hills with goats
and bells, an old chestnut,
a turtle on the edge of the footpath
making soft crumpling noises.

THE MOUSE AND THE HUMAN

The mouse doesn't really bother anyone. It doesn't
go around holding up banks or shooting people
in the face or locking them up in dank jail cells
and sticking electric prods to their genitals. It doesn't
build jet fighters and bomb our cities in the name
of peace in the middle of the night while we are sleeping.
It doesn't plant toy mines to blow our children's arms off.
All the mouse wants is to share with us some shelter,
food, even the warmth of its nervous body. Yet we plug up
the cupboards so it can't eat, and we chase it around
the living room with a broom and remove all the chairs
till it has nowhere to hide; then we club it to death
as it squeals. Or we set up traps with something it likes
to lure it into strangulation and burst its eyes out
of its head. And against what? A few light scratchings
heard in the ceiling once in a while keeping us company
at night? Two or three crumbs of bread taken from
the kitchen floor? And after the mouse, there are the ants
to be poisoned, the bees to be gassed and burned.
Later, the dandelions to be choked by spraying. And after
that, after that, there must be something after that.

SURVEILLANCE

At the shoe store, the girl
behind the counter
looks inside each shoe
for socks or polish I may have
stolen. I don't take it
personally, not a matter of trust.
She is doing her job,
like bagging or whistling
casually, her eyes searching each
shoe. Still, I see her wondering,
see her awareness of me
watching her search,
amid my awareness of her
searching, that she might find
what she is looking for.
On the news, in this period
of surveillance, commentators say
if you have nothing to hide,
there's nothing to worry about.
She hands me the bag and we smile
a checkout smile, and the bell
by the door rings as I leave.

is one question; what about this:
you walk around with a wound;
people look at you, knowing;
they've been talking; word has spread;
the talking needs fuel; and your hiding
leads to more talk; they spot you,
passing on the street; they look,
trying to see something they can use;
people are wired to do that;
and it works; they say your name
and, in the meantime, hello.

enslaved, yet saves exactly who I am
I don't want to give you an example—
it's too private, I think, painful—
Let's talk about the weather, how
humid it is these days, or
the war—why we are always at war,
or let's not talk. Is there a quietness
that can make us whole?

CALM SPRING DAY

I prefer a place where there is nothing,
he said, no people walking dogs,

no children laughing, no trees, no shade,

somewhere where you can't see the other side.
He paced Lake Ontario's shore, listening

to the sea of it, watching light
off the water, and in the air

the smell of rotting shellfish, and toward land
the decks of summer homes,
windows still boarded up.

IN NEW YORK CITY

We were exceedingly friendly
with many strangers. In the pastry shops
or anywhere—mostly in eateries,
I noticed. People asked our names,
started conversation, looked at us,
as we at them, with hunger for the idea
of sex, or some contact. Once or twice,
an angel's wing came, lifted us,
amidst our looking, into something
more serene, slightly surprising us
and the strangers, at the time of our parting.

FROM MOUNT ATHOS

I pick strawberries in the garden. Three long rows
behind the monastery, before the midday sun gets too hot.
I set down a stool every few yards and reach out
my hands, first for what is visible, then shake
and lift the leaves for fruit and color.
With a slight pull, I test each berry's readiness
for being plucked, having found
my rhythm in the field. All morning
I fill a blue crate, carry it to the refectory, then rest
in my cell to the sound of cicadas and flies
through the open window.
The evening dessert is red glistening strawberries,
piled onto shining metal plates, next to glasses
of wine, vases of water, whole tomatoes,
bean soup, fresh bread, olives: others' work,
all set on a common table.
Afterward, from high on the balcony, the Aegean
ripples with infinite small lights, the trees
of the mountain move like the sea, the air brings
a mixed scent of pine and iodine and night.
Beauty is more evident in this quiet. You see it
through a clearing inside yourself. It is no mystery, seeing.

DELIVERY

I knock, standing on the unadorned
cement steps separated from the dull red
ranch. Come in, she says, I've been waiting
for you, Dear. She orders a grinder and lottery
tickets and Camel cigarettes. The television
is on, playing midday game shows, the picture
faded green. It's an old furniture model
with wooden legs and fuzzed-up golden threads
over the speaker. There are photos on top:
the husband who died, the kids who don't visit,
one of them down South. Pill bottles are knocked
over on the lamp stand, amid scattered change
and lipstick half out of its tube. Someone should
clean this place, someone should come by, I'm
thinking. She sits sunk into the couch and reaches
for the cigarettes first, breaks open one fresh
pack, gets the new smoke inside her till she's more
at ease. Put the tickets on the stand, she says.
Put the grinder on the table in the kitchen.
Her kids told her to stop smoking. She has a bad
heart, and the doctor told her to stop, but she'll be
damned if she'll quit the only thing left she likes.
She asks me about school and how we make
our meatballs—about anything. After a while, I find
a space and say, well, and she continues talking.
Well, I say, I better get back to the pizza place.
You're leaving, Dear? I'll see you
soon, I say, and fumble toward the door,
down the steps, and onto the bare winter lawn.

THE PACKAGE STORE

People come in for six-packs,
cigarettes, Powerball tickets, or to redeem
their empties. We talk about nothing,
or we look each other in the eye
too hard, or not at all, or with an earnestness
bound to money. Some say nothing
without words, but move from the cooler
to the counter leaving a streak
of determined silence, indecipherable.
With others, a mysterious brightness forms
around us for a short time, and we are held
in that light, during the exchange
of dollars, or the clutch of a bottle from hand
to hand. When that person leaves, I sit alone,
barren, peaceful, safe with no one,
as on a sunny windless day in an empty parking lot.
Then, another car pulls in. I get up
off the chair and with my right palm clear
the counter of imaginary dust, a vestige
of a gesture used in invocations once to beg
for grace.

PRAYING OR LOVE POEM

I go to the bookstore, where I don't
want to go, especially, or to be, after I get there,

as if being is burdensome, as if I might find a place
to set it down, instead of carrying it,

so I can rest. Perhaps I mean the body's
weight and entire containment,

the soul straining and fatigued.

The bookstore, in afternoon light, with comforting
jazz, a cafe, people absorbed

in reading and in conversation, is not the place
I want to find. Nor will the next place be

where I go dragging that weight as if I had chosen it
as a solemn and mysterious duty.

I HAVE TWO WHITE STONES
(after Tomaz Salamun)

I have two white stones on my dresser. I picked them by the shore of a
      monastery in
Greece and brought them with me to America. I hope they are not sad.
I have a white car with rust. My mother made red seat covers for the red seats.
I have a green shirt that runs when I wash it. I wear it to exercise.
I have a raw throb around one tooth. I put my tongue on the flesh's rawness.
I have loneliness. Loneliness and I walk together, back and forth to school. And
      we are so
peaceful together.
I have old coins my father gave me and I have his glasses in a drawer. Some
      things I keep
and keep.
I have a friend. She is beautiful. I want to tell you, her name is Irena.
I have a book my mother gave me, with a beautiful black horse and a boy on
      the cover,
with purple blue background and mountains. It is the only book she ever
gave me. She doesn't read.
I have walking. Walking is like the air and the sky and the stars whenever I
      need them.
Or like the sun on your back, or on your face, or through a window on a
      bed in a
room where you've gone to read the letter in the quiet house, or like the
      smell of
the sun on your arm, or like touching your nose on the hair on your arm
      to smell,
even on a cold day.

THE THIRD ONE
(after Yannis Ritsos)

Three men walked
by the side of the lake
Easter Sunday.
The water was still.
Their body language
spoke broken English.
It rolled its gestures
and made them seem
like newly arrived immigrants,
somewhat out of place.
The first one arched his hands
like domes of great civilizations
when he talked,
and swung his intentions
hard through the air.
The second one's laughter
was an open
market by the seaside,
streaming with the smell of freshly
killed fish and the misty smack
of vendors' voices.
The sky filled more
with his laughter
than it does with ours.
The third and closest
to the water
simply walked
with his head turned toward
the shore, taking in the skim and whisper
of geese crossing the sunset.
He was like a passenger

on a long bus ride,
quiet in the inside seat,
watching towns pulsate and disappear
through breath-fogged windows.

BONE MARROW BIOPSY

Time moves very slowly
in the hospital: a clock

high on the corridor
wall, an empty chair

by the window, nurses
passing in the rhythm of

their work, the color white,
red. The wheels of my mother's

bed swivel and lock. She wears
a tan gown, her regular

clothes tucked in a plastic
bag. The tools are arranged

on a tray. Time slows more
during the procedure. When

we walk to the car, the morning
outside is otherwise blue and clear.

"Think of it this way," he said.
"You have a lawn,
and you have dandelions on that lawn.
You can use a little herbicide at a time,
so after a while, the dandelions reappear;
or you can use a lot of herbicide all at once,
and risk damaging your lawn,
or you can pave the entire lawn over
with asphalt."

Then I took my mother and we left.
We stopped at our favorite hot dog shop
to order our usual: one plain dog for her,
two chili for me, and fries to share.
We went back home and ate together
at the kitchen table: two glasses of water
and napkins with children holding hands.

THE TREE

Because of the morning bird singing,
song will persist inside me.
Because of the sound of traffic,
I shall always wonder,
and I shall be troubled at what remains
unknown. But I shall hope. And because of the mailbox,
and the road, and the tree. It is hard to despair
because of the tree. Slowly, we turn toward love.

she wants to hear. We communicate
back and forth by agreeing
on things. "These potatoes are tasty,"
I say. "I told you," she says,
"the potatoes they sell at the bottom
of the mountain are the best."
"Nice breeze," I say. "Mmm," she says.
I like listening to some sweetness
in her voice as we sit in our yard
in the village after her stroke,
amid the bees, sparrows,
the grape vines, the plum tree,
the butterflies, while we wait
under the great blue sky, in the shade,
for the fish to cook, amid the midday light,
the penetrating heat, some gray
lizards nearby, the rusted dustpan,
the feeding pot for the cats,
a frayed straw broom up against the door
to the old kitchen.

RETURNING FROM GREECE

A deep blue luminous dye surrounds the edges
of the land. Hours later, we touch down in New York.
The water is gray. We are tired
and begin to forget, again. Without
knowing it, we march off in the various directions.

THE MAN WITH THE FLYING CAR

He was flying a car which he landed on a smooth, wavy surface.
The car turned into a bicycle, and he pedaled hard
over a bridge with many people walking on it. Some of the people
were walking faster than he was pedaling, though it didn't seem
they were in a rush. Then, he was back at the house
by the water, though he didn't recognize that water, nor that house,
aside from a familiarity one feels with strange places. His brother
had come from a long way to pick him up, and there was another
man in that house, but the flier of the car didn't visit
his brother and the other man. His first instinct was discomfort.
He stayed in another room, the next room, playing a board game
by himself, knowing how to be, mostly, that way.

MEETING

Fifteen years.
My father dead.

I've seen him since. Once.
In a dream.

Obscured by blood. Smiling
through blood.

Speaking with the smile of an
amputated beggar. I was

afraid of his armless embrace.
I kept moving away. Afraid

of turning into mutilated
limbs myself. Trailing after

others, who run in fear.
He remembers

me afraid, loveless,
and hasn't returned.

NOT FOR A REASON

Tonight at the train station
with the red metal seats
in Syracuse. We walked up the ramp,
then beyond the few people
on the platform. I wasn't looking
at her legs, though I've taken the shape
of her knees into my palms before,
followed from heel to calf, up and up,
she being my future wife, maybe,
though we keep saying yes,
and I should say yes here, not maybe,
because she and I both believe
strongly, but people have believed before
and still it has stopped being.
The train came, left.
I walked from beyond the few
people on the platform (who had gone
by then) where we had been,
holding. Legs can't look off into a distance
somewhere, as eyes can,
filled with thinking something unthought.
Legs can do that, too, walking
in cemeteries, back to the car, through fog,
even when there is no distance.

NO MATTER WHAT

In America, if you have a car, and you aren't
too sad, you can still drive on the highway
in August with the windows rolled down
on a muggy night, passing green signs with white
letters, taking in the soft rubbery scent of air,
perhaps thinking about what cannot be unraveled,

like when you were little and had just come over
on a plane from somewhere else for the first time,
landed in a New York airport, an uncle there
to pick you up, everything new and swirling,
and that same fleshy air, like the air you
walk through in the city at night after wine,
everything sticky and bright, almost alive.

LOVE NOTE

I have last night
to thank for this writing,
not so much for the material
as for the exhaustion
which brings quietness
and burning eyes
to reconfigure vision,
somehow, and song happens.
Thank you, last night,
and the people downstairs
hating each other.
Thank you, too, for letting me
sleep in your bed,
for turning it sideways
and adding couch cushions
where our feet were
to make the space wider
so I could breathe
and be with you
at the same time.

A PERFECT DAY

"What?" he said.
"Sit down under this tree
and what?"

I said, "I want
to read you a poem."

He was my brother
and we never
did things like that.

It was Sunday afternoon
blue and cloudless;
we sat underneath

a maple in our backyard,
and halfway through the poem,
we began to cry.

It was good practice
for what we never do.

WATERING

Watering the dahlias at midnight tonight,
and a certain rose bush that goes dry every year,
after the first bloom. I'm trying to change its fate
if possible.

The weather report says hot and humid for tomorrow,
highs nearing one hundred degrees.

On the front steps:
basil, a mosquito plant,
tomatoes, geraniums,
pansies by the walkway,
irises and snapdragons I planted with my mother.

Some will need to be moved
to keep from being burned.

The news says talks break down over Kosovo,
bombings to be ratcheted up.

I will water them all.
It hasn't rained for a long time.

By the tap at the side of the house
and late into the hours of dark,
I move about the yard prayerfully,
filling and refilling the pail.

SIESTA

A mild wind rustles the fig tree in the full sun
of an open lot at the far end of the noontime street.
Loose cinder blocks lie unarranged in a corner
next to a pile of limestone powder
by the half-finished wall of a new house.
A sifting screen leans against a wheelbarrow,
and moist mortar dries between bricks.

After lunch, neighborhood cats gather
in the yard underneath the canopy of grape leaves.
The worker's wife emerges, unfolding
her apron, dropping crumbs of bread and cheese,
bits of potato soaked in olive oil, and tasty bones
of red mullet, whose eyes just that morning
filled with the sway and crimson of sea anemones.

AGORA

We buy olives in the market on Saturdays.
The taxi drivers line up. The girls walk through,
holding their mothers' arms. The Russian merchants
sell binoculars and snake oil and bits of pieces of trees
that cure everything. The old women gather round,
crowding the counter, pushing sideways to look in.
A man selling leeks and cabbage adjusts his scale.
The fishermen are at the very end: the cold smell
of ice and salt and fresh blood on soiled hard hands
stains the wet concrete floor.

COMMERCE

The logging trucks haul dead elephant limbs
through the gentle town.
They pass the flag of the memorial green in the rain.
The road is tired and cold.
The marching band has stopped for the season.
The people watch from their windows.

MAGIC VOICE

People call who don't know me and ask for my dead father
by his first name. I tell them he's not in.
When they ask for the best time to call, I say, "Now,
he's usually here." I've begun to hang up on them,
contributing to the collapse of feeling. More and more, machines
call, offering services and solutions. Today, one from Magic
Kitchens, dispensing something in a man's voice.

Sometimes, when I'm watching sporting events on TV
and the owners of the clubs are shown (behind glass boxes—
philanthropic, the announcers often say, referring perhaps
to time spent with inner-city kids), I think of popular
peasant uprisings that are squashed, and non-compliant
countries bombed for years, populations starved
and diseased to death, and when I hear words like *democracy*
on the TV, or *human rights*, or words that seem opposite:
genocide, *weapons of mass destruction*, *terrorism*,
I picture the noble faces of the team owners, and everything
makes more sense. Or just before we bomb other countries,
when anchormen speak of the lavish palaces of enemy dictators.

THE LITTLE BOX AS LESS THAN ABSOLUTE
(after Vasko Popa)

Numbered, in the basement of a library,
with hinges, a keyhole, wooden,
a small plastic see-through space;
or in a train station, metal and locked,
where someone in a movie left
a final clue before he died;
or my "cubbie" in sixth grade.

There is nothing especially sacred
about the little box. You can't hide it
or what's in it with any great sense
of integrity. If your house were a box
and you were hiding Jews behind
a secret door, the Germans
could easily demolish it into fine splinters,
regardless of your words. And it wouldn't
have to be the Germans. It could be you,
me, our eyes for a split-second
meeting as we avoid the pain.

ENDURING FREEDOM

The man in the boldly decorated military suit
is a four-star general. A family of eight in Kabul
is eating breakfast. He is showing green
night-cam video clips of targets and operations
to handpicked reporters. A bomb tears through
the family's roof and kills them. The reporters
ask limp, polite questions. A three-year-old girl,
her five-year-old sister, four brothers, parents.
A humorous moment occurs at the news conference.
A bomb tears through her house. Something
causes the General to smile, and, following his cue,
reporters smile and even raise their voices
in obedient containments of laughter. The bazaars
in Kandahar are bombed. The General says
he has no numbers. Two brothers walking far
from the market carts are hit by spraying
shrapnel in their faces, stomachs, legs, arms. The news
conference concludes. A man in some distress then
asks about a remedy for heartburn. Car financing
is discussed. I push the button and go outside
to the sky full blue, the October foliage brilliant.
I have no appetite. My legs walk me.

BY THE PIER

Vistas of people walking
by the pier tonight, and seagulls
dipping at the smooth sheet,
and harbor lights casting fire glows
on the water. The sound of bicycle bells
as they pass, and the smell of corn
roasting on top of charcoal,
and the swinging legs of children,
perfectly illogical pendulums,
back and forth over the ocean.

EARLY APRIL EVENING

Instead of writing a poem
about writing a poem,
I decide to open
the window.

The spring air is growing warmer and more elastic.
I hear girls in tank tops
off in the semi-distance
driving for the shore
windows rolled down
music flowing like their hair
and the sound of night tires
licking the moistening road.

CONVERSION

Any minute now, amid this heightened, contrived
talk, making of art, trying, prayer. I think
in confused puddles, like a prisoner, or shattered bird,
and that it can be no other way.

Something should break, or deepen, once you decide
to say no and no and no, or from irrational force, say it:
finally you are alone, and everything is landscape,
whatever sense you might get out of that, substituted

for people, interchangeable. People, landscape, ideas.
The mailbox, the woman in spring, the field of clover.

the playwright said. Our mentality, psyche, have altered,
to undignified, shameless, ungenerous, mean,
inhospitable, rude, indelicate, discourteous, quibbling,
prevaricating, poor fellow-beings.

Sometimes I drive late at night to the supermarket,
alone, and walk the aisles of plenty, take ice cream, thin
spaghetti, pass the sex of lights and persons,
or out past everything. Still no solution.

That awkward moment
when someone you know walks by
pretending he doesn't see you.

It's happening now.
A man I know is coming out of the library
and though I'd rather not speak with him,
I continue looking
in order to draw his attention.

Based on our previous encounters
my guess is that, if he does look back,
I'll say, "Hey Mike,"
and he'll give his usual index finger flick
and simultaneous nod of the head
while continuing on his way.

Things got like this after we had lunch once
and I discovered he was a right wing fascist
who feels "we" should be in Iraq etc., keeping the world
safe, and so on. He discovered me to be an irrational,
commie, leftist, saboteur of the republic, etc.,
enemy of the empire, and so on.

Those impressions have proved lasting.

Now his head is slightly bowed
as he passes me.
No point in yelling out his name.
He rounds a corner and slowly, methodically,
raises his head

to take in the view of people more openly,
though still protective,
disguised, feigning aloofness, as if in denial
of taking them in, as if he suspects
someone is watching.

MEDITATION IN SPRING

Year after year it comes, or most years it does, though you can't plan for it.
Some day in March, when the cold finally breaks, 50 degrees and melting snow,
but quiet. Quiet in the yard, quiet on the school grounds. And huge distant
whirls of traffic, machinery of buildings, turbines of the world. The grass not
yet green. The air against your hair, your face, the sun warm there. A car now
and then over the silver gold water. A distant siren. Someone having passed you
turning to look back. The quality of light in March that says life is passing.
The white salt on the street from winter. The fire hydrant and its shadow.
It comes, this awareness. You hear buses passing. Crows and other birds
in the sky you sometimes forget. The splendor and death of buildings,
smokestacks, satellite dishes. A streak of jet fuel in the 4 p.m. sky. The air
leafing through your notebook with impossible fingers. The smell of city
fuel and food and sweet garbage. How infrequently, how poorly one wonders.
That it takes a change of light, and sitting, and, mostly, the time for any of it.
The still mind. The seagull as spectacular, singular, passing. Though you can't
plan for it. The diminishing piles of snow, small, and their wet shadows.

ABORTED INSTRUCTIONS

Make sure that a poem resists answering its questions
to keep yourself and the poem from false knowledge—

better somehow that you remain oblivious
to whether a question has even been raised, until you discover it

unexpectedly, with pleasure, while rereading your poem,
and find yourself wondering how the question got there, emerged

then into your mind, skin, soul, what was right for that to happen,
bringing sunlight to radiate on the page, the letters become trees,

people, chickens, a church and its yard, five mountains:
the sudden appearance and activity of life and your perception of it

with a clear eye, and an attendant emotion of great liberation,
from routine, from past, from self.

But what have you done to bring about vision?
You've been incidental the entire time, chosen, not free.

ADVICE FOR POEMS

The budding tree in spring believes your poems should catch shreds of plastic
      bags on their branches to blow like graceful flags.
The pine cone on the ground believes your poems need nothing, not even
        to wait,
      for that which happens will always, has always, is.
The grackle on the hill believes your poems need to search for feed
      and also stop, to stare at the wind or the sky.
The wind believes your poems need to be known, and never to be known.
The three sparrows chasing each other, playing, believe your poems need to be
      making first lines always.
The round and coned evergreen believes your poems do not move but for
        the wind
      and the squirrel at their limbs and the continuous growth which can be
      seen only through long blinks.
The fly believes your poems need to appear, seemingly, out of nowhere,
      to land on a hand and temper that hand's patience.
The crows believe your poems need to appear suddenly by the reader's
        right shoulder
      and arc down the shape of the hill, their bodies barely audible in the air.
The squirrel believes your poems need to climb up and down trees, frenetically,
        sometimes,
      and dig into the soil, with nerves vibrating the tail, and pause,
      motionless, then look up, then about, at grass level.
The grass on the hill believes your poems need nothing, that every year,
        whatever is
      needed is provided; the trees believe this, too, that are neither happy
      nor sad,
      nor have faith or are faithless, nor do they know or not know, but
      are, exist.
The small needle that falls from the tree believes your poems need to fall from
        the tree,
      that the earth will catch them, that they might become earth.

THERE IS A WINDOW IN MAINE,

open, in the dark
of June, to a field, a marsh
with peepers, one or two
tree silhouettes, stars.
And the air comes in waves
at the curtain and touches
its hand on our faces,
as we lie in bed, the kind
of air that says:
you will remember this
window, this caress,
the curtain soft, rustling.

Is never having kissed best?
Does touching once or, better yet, almost once
make the touching more intense?
When I sit by any shore and gaze out
into emptiness, and listen to the sweet howl
of silence, I remember and feel all
the events of my life, each one.
The lost and unattained ones
feel most attained, most pleasurable, though
there's work in this for me, too: I must keep them
(as keeping's the important part) by desire, alive,
in a drawer, an envelope, or by the whole sea.
The waves go in and out of me
as if I were transparent, a vessel, or barely there.

A NON-ARGUMENT

We spend life hiding. The mind tightens; then pressure
collapses it—alcohol against pain, for example—
and the impulse is to say there will be flowers, but the floor
remains cluttered, though the music persists in every
scrap of the undivided, complete universe.
The story goes back and forth: tonight a man violently
staggers across a lawn, and he lets fall from his shoulder
a beautiful metal guitar to crash.

Someone pays with ten singles;
after him someone with more
singles just as I am
nearly out. Or the beer brands
I'm short on don't get bought,
and everything runs low
so evenly you'd think someone
was regulating all this. Even
love feels provident some
days, like beers or money,
and, some days, like we've been
damned from the beginning.

CORNERS OF WINDOWS

One self went on and had children
who played in the summer yard
and a happy wife.

Another self fucked as many women
as he could and lived in the wild barren
light someone called freedom,
with art and seashells and a terribly endless sky.

One self tried to know God.

Many died from love.

The rest stayed by the corners
of windows looking out into afternoon streets
with shaded basketball hoops,
women pushing carriages,

silent howling green swaying trees,
very full in late June.

These selves, waiting for what cannot come
by the corners of windows.
Not waiting. Mourning.

HUNGER STRIKE

We didn't believe her when she said it hurts,
because the tests kept coming back fine.

The doctor said it was nothing to be alarmed at,
and that, mostly, it was a lack of courage—

or stress. She said only each person knows
what he or she has, when we told her to have

courage, and that there was worse out there,
and to be patient, and not burden others

when she felt weak. When she said she couldn't,
and that she was losing herself from the world,

and to pray for her, we thought she was
overdoing it. We didn't know what to tell her

anymore. No one understands me, she said.

there is nothing left to do wherever I am,
my despair opens

the shutters of its house and begins
to lean out and peer over the town

and pour out into it.

It is frightening, but strange
that the trees in sun, in shade, in wind,

the rocks, the hill, feel as my despair
does then, though they all remain

mysterious and beautiful, perfect.
The people are more

ambiguous, though my despair
casts itself over them, too.

The people are outright hopeful,
some electrified

strain of hope coursing in their bodies,
rendering them almost comic, absurd,

immune to my despair, questioning it,

in their hats, haircuts, clothing, intention,
jagged and musical walks.

AFFINITIES

It is afternoon. White sand. Gulls. A sharp wind in late September.
A woman with a blue bikini top throws on a flannel shirt.

Shafts of sun fan through the clouds. The wind blasts the helpless
short trees. We've come on a drive, past farm houses—

we could live there—and fields of mowed-down corn. American flags
and plastic pumpkin statues on lawns. Soon it will be Halloween,

Thanksgiving, Christmas, then Happy New Year's, again.
We've moved two picnic tables with benches attached, set them

parallel to the lake, separated by twenty feet or so. You paint.
I write. The sound of water and air between us, wonderfully.

The sky darkens. Metallic blue. And the wind picks up more.
Suddenly it is cold. Suddenly autumn begins, while we're sitting there,

with goose bumps, no longer enjoying ourselves, holding fast
to the benches and tables, but waiting, a bit longer, before we go.

My mother is talking to someone while she half sleeps
on the couch in the living room. She has stopped
sleeping in her room and moved to the more open,
more exposed space now that she's the only one
in the house. Her way of trying to scare off fear,
I think, to gain an advantage. In my village,
people nearing the gates of death often begin to talk
with those who have already crossed into that place.
The little I know of this: from my great aunt when
she was dying. People on the other side are usually
okay. During one of her visits, she saw and spoke
with my father, told us he was at peace. I can't hear
my mother clearly from my room, but there is tension,
a sense in her voice and phrasing, of mild asphyxiation.
I can't tell who she is talking to, or what it is about.

QUESTIONS FOR MY DEAD AUNT IN THE VILLAGE

Is there a ring around the moon? Has the weather spoiled?
Have the rains begun? Did you stop gathering wood
as the mountains became dark and the sky opened up?
Have chimneys begun to breathe? Is the church quieter?
Is it cold there Sundays? Do the windows fog?
When it snows, will you still go? Will you sit by the fire?
Have you lifted and secured the latch? Do you hear
the dogs in the dark, as you lie under thick wool blankets?
What of the yards, the houses, when spring comes?
Are the neighborhoods alive? Does anyone tell stories late
into the night? Were there mushrooms this year? Who went?

SERVICE

And not only the work of daytime and picking strawberries
but the work of the first hours deep in night,
when the air is new on the windows, when the wood is first struck
(when the word is first struck) calling you from your cell
to rise and dress and throw water on your face
and walk, as if for the first time, taking uneven steps,
a small flashlight guiding your way down the wood stairs
onto the stone and grass and uneven perfection of the courtyard,
below the clarity of stars, the brilliant black sky,
in the pre-dawn coolness, as you enter the chapel,
candlelight slowly growing from the icons,
sound from the reverential stones, and you stand in time, time
not as measurement but as quality, in the great scent of quiet,
praying there, praying through to daylight, and beyond.

SIN

Everything is possible for the person who has faith.
But what if you're not cut out for sitting across the table
from others, having sane, sensible, extended discussions
on literature, art, world affairs, being natural that way,
nodding, joking, crossing your legs, sipping, looking,
taking a drag, a bite—what people do? In the Bible,
there is an image of someone with a large millstone tied
around his neck, sinking in the sea. How it feels,
finally, to suck in the whole sea in one breath, become
overtaken by it, inverted by it, as with love, drowning.

Just now I am thinking of an unfinished poem I wrote
years ago, about calling to a woman after
she decided to walk away. The wind kept turning
my voice back on itself. There was a hill in the poem
the woman was walking down, and a spring
that wasn't in the picture of the poem—it was
a destination she had set out for, and there were two
water jugs, which she had left, and almonds,
which also couldn't be seen, but were to be picked,
and a coat, which wasn't in the poem's picture either,
but which the woman had forgotten to take, and an apron—
in the poem I called it: her gathering apron.
In the case of that poem, the wind pushing my voice
back on itself would be the thing which persists
for me. The hill persists, too. Or a field. My mother
had a dream of me walking in a bright green field.
She said it was a good dream, and I've held
onto that view, that field, which, if my life were a poem,
would be visible in the picture of the poem, though
perhaps not only as a literal field. But it would be my mother's
dream itself, in the picture of my life, in a corner
or anywhere, shining deeply and brightly and quietly,
like an icon. And more than the dream itself.
It would be the dreaming, her dreaming.

MY MOTHER'S ROOM

The whitish gray jacket she wore
to my graduation hangs
on the closet knob.
I kiss its shoulder
with soft slow steady lips
and touch the shoulder with my palm
each time I enter here
to smell, or just to wonder.
Four suitcases here,
and two more in the village.
Small cheap locks
latched onto the zippers.
A braided orange yarn handle
replacing the broken one
and leather belts from the village cobbler
to strap around the belly's load.
She used to wish the suitcases
might stay together in one place,
or—better—that they'd never been bought,
lugging and dispersing hope as they did
back and forth across the ocean
all those years, her lost name
etched deep into their sides.

RAIN

The foreboding, suspended darkness
and thick air of the woods before rain begins
to gather. A lonely place, where days
are days again, and you listen to your life
as if it were a poem, the dark residence
of silence and clockless time. The you
you don't know through knowing is waiting
to find and to be found, to search
and to bloom. Then back to the car,
as the drops begin on the roof and more
silent drops on your leg with the door open,
becoming fat, steady, heavy, the rain.

FORMS

I've been a ghost many times, in my own skin. I've returned
to summer villages by the sea, balconies and curtains filled with sea air,
breakfasts of fresh peach, cheese, bread, and water,
the smell of warmth on bodies timelessly resting in the sun, sunlight
on bodies, ripening the bodies. I've walked on the sand by the blue-green sea,
lain in the radiant warmth of coves for centuries at a time,
among ancient stones, pine and sea fragrance. At night, past glowing cafes
and glowing faces, I've walked beyond village lights,
to promontories, and sat at the base of shrines and stared out
in the direction of the endless, toward what I could not see,
which seemed to me the most familiar, the most common and intimate
thing and place I had ever known. And one time with a beautiful woman,
by the edge and very heart of a village, the sea steadily rose and took in
          our feet.
Touch had made the world invisible, or had confirmed its true invisibility,
then. The wind was cool and warm. At once her hair was on my lips.

left unmowed by one of the groundskeepers.
When I pause, in bright morning light, the color
transforms me
into itself. Or I transform it,
or God does. Who can tell?
And how can I tell you
about the mullein's reflection
on the still water. I believe because of this
joy we might meet.

I WILL SWEEP

What will you do in the village alone in the house
with your mother gone in autumn with winter coming?
I will sleep with the terrifying and brave blackness at night
of the village and of the house. I will sweep the yard
of plum leaves and pear leaves, with the short broom,
my back bent. Sweep, clean, tidy up, my arm repeating
a motion until I am woven with my dead into a clear
and living braid. Then I will sit in one of the chairs
by the white table and wait on the wind, the birds,
the ancient scent of the house, joyous and crying.